JAMES McNAIR'S
Cold Cuisine

Photography by Patricia Brabant

Chronicle Books • San Francisco

Printed in Japan

Library of Congress
Cataloging in Publication Data
McNair, James K.
James McNair's Cold Cuisine;
Includes index.
1. Cookery (Cold dishes) I. Title
II. Title: Cold cuisine.
TX830.M33 1988
641.7'9
88-2578

ISBN 0-87701-501-5
ISBN 0-87701-487-6 (pbk.)

Distributed in Canada by
Raincoast Books
112 East Third Avenue
Vancouver, British Columbia V5T 1C8

10 9 8 7 6 5 4 3 2 1

Chronicle Books
San Francisco, California

To Elvin McDonald who placed me in my first design job in New York
two decades ago, then a few years later, in California, hired me for my first
writing assignment, and who has remained a mentor and friend through the
years.

And to John Carr, a relatively new friend and extended family member,
with thanks for all the things he shares so generously with me, especially
his Eagle Street kitchen and the pets.

Produced by The Rockpile Press, San Francisco and Lake Tahoe

**Art direction, photographic and food styling, and book design
by James McNair**

Editorial production assistance by Lin Cotton

Studio kitchen assistance by Gail High and Mary Val McCoy

Recipe testing assistance by Mary Val McCoy

Photography assistance by Shari Cohen and Seth Affoumado

Typography and mechanical production by CTA Graphics

contents

introduction

Among my happiest memories of several years spent in New Orleans are the frequent shrimp boils shared with a few close friends. On warm days when the almost overwhelming fragrance of nearby sweet olives perfumed the humid air, a couple of us would walk over to one of the fish markets just inside the levee that separates the Mississippi from the old French Market and buy piles of fresh shrimp for very little money. Back in one of our French Quarter flats, we'd cook them up in spicy crab boil, then chill them. At supper time we'd spread the kitchen table with several layers of *The Times-Picayune*, mound the cold shrimp in the middle, and put out individual containers of dipping sauce. Peeling at the table made for messy eating, but the results were sheer ecstasy! I've included a recipe for a similar cold feast in this book.

At the other end of the cold food presentation scale, I fondly remember several impromptu European picnics enjoyed with my partner Lin Cotton a decade ago. We'd buy fancy cold fare, usually highly garnished and coated in shiny aspic, from such food emporiums as Fauchon in Paris, Pecks in Milan, or the Food Halls of Harrods in London. We'd enjoy our selections in nearby parks, or once in a rowboat while drifting on the Grand Canal of Versailles. Such upscale cuisine intended to be eaten cold or at room temperature is represented in this book by Pork and Ham Pâté in Pastry, Duck Galantine, and Scallop and Salmon Mousses.

A year or so after that particular European jaunt, Lin and I opened Twin Peaks Gourmet in San Francisco. After serving up what seemed like tons of rich cold delicacies, both of us, along with our dogs, overdosed from eating up the overstock. With some distance from that experience, I can once again enjoy Layered Vegetable Terrine, Jellied Beef, or country-style Veal and Pork Terrine and have included them among the recipes. In addition to these and a few other time-consuming elaborate creations, I've included in this book some of my favorite simple cold dishes such as Sashimi, Marinated Squid, and Stuffed Eggplant, Turkish Style.

The varied dishes in this book share the common requirement that they be thoroughly chilled prior to serving. This doesn't mean that you'll necessarily eat them cold, for most chilled foods are at their best when they've returned almost to room temperature.

Upon reading a recipe, you may think I've suggested too much seasoning. Keep in mind that a lot of subtle flavors that would be present in hot foods are lost in the chilling process. To assure a flavorful final product, I recommend overseasoning a bit when you taste before refrigerating.

Except for a few sweet treats at the end, most dishes in this recipe collection can serve either as starters—appetizers or first courses—or as the main event, depending upon the portion served and the accompaniments. Or they can be grouped together to form perfect fare for warm weather outings or buffet parties at any season. Some dishes may become your favorite take-alongs for potlucks or other food-sharing events. Best of all, each dish is made well ahead of serving time, allowing the flavors to blend and mellow and a relaxed cook to serve them with ease.

Golden Gazpacho

Yellow tomatoes and golden peppers create a new look for an old favorite, although red tomatoes and peppers can substitute. In any case, be sure the tomatoes are ripe and flavorful.

Peel, seed, and chop the tomatoes. Place them in a food processor or blender, add the garlic, coarsely chopped pepper, coarsely chopped cucumber, sherry vinegar, 3 tablespoons of the olive oil, and salt and pepper to taste. Purée until fairly smooth. Transfer to a bowl, cover, and refrigerate for at least 4 hours or as long as overnight. Let stand at room temperature for about 15 minutes before serving.

Preheat the oven to 350° F.

To make croutons for garnish, combine the 3 remaining tablespoons of the olive oil with the minced garlic in a bowl. Add the bread cubes and toss to coat thoroughly. Spread on a baking sheet and bake until light brown. Remove from the oven and reserve.

To serve, stir the soup and ladle it into individual bowls and add a sprinkling of each garnish, or pass the garnishes for adding to taste at the table.

Serves 6 as a starter, or 2 or 3 as a main course.

2½ pounds ripe yellow tomatoes
3 garlic cloves
1 cup coarsely chopped golden sweet pepper
1 cup peeled and coarsely chopped English cucumber
3 tablespoons sherry vinegar or white wine vinegar
6 tablespoons olive oil, preferably extra-virgin
Salt
Freshly ground black pepper
1 teaspoon minced or pressed garlic, or to taste
3 slices French bread, trimmed of crusts and cut into ¼-inch cubes
Peeled, seeded, and chopped or sliced yellow tomato for garnish
Minced fresh chives for garnish
Peeled and diced English cucumber for garnish
Fresh lemon thyme for garnish (optional)
Pesticide-free yellow edible flowers or petals such as calendula, French marigolds, or nasturtiums for garnish (optional)

Stuffed Eggplant, Turkish Style
(Imam Bayildi)

2 large eggplants
Coarse salt
About ¾ cup olive oil, preferably
    extra-virgin
3 medium-sized yellow onions,
    finely chopped
3 large ripe tomatoes, peeled, seeded
    if desired, and chopped
3 or 4 garlic cloves, minced or pressed
3 tablespoons minced fresh parsley
3 tablespoons freshly squeezed
    lemon juice
½ teaspoon granulated sugar
Freshly ground black pepper

The Turkish name for this dish translates "the priest fainted." Legend has it that he swooned from ecstasy upon tasting the dish, although other theories maintain that his sinking spell occurred when he learned how much precious olive oil had been used in the dish.

This has been my favorite eggplant presentation since first sampling it in New York years ago at a tiny hole-in-the-wall restaurant where Hussan, the owner-chef, prepared it as below. Since then I've found numerous recipes that call for whole or halved eggplants, but I still prefer thick slices for a more elegant presentation.

Discard the blossom ends from the eggplants and cut the unpeeled vegetable lengthwise into slices ¾ inch thick. Lay the slices on paper toweling and sprinkle with salt to draw out excess moisture. Cover with paper toweling and a heavy weight and let stand for 30 minutes.

Heat ¼ cup of the olive oil in a large sauté pan or skillet over medium-high heat and sauté the onions until soft but not brown, about 5 minutes. Add the tomatoes, garlic, parsley, lemon juice, sugar, and salt and pepper to taste. Sauté for 2 or 3 minutes longer. Reserve.

Preheat the oven to 350° F.

Using paper toweling, blot moisture from the eggplant slices. To create a pocket in each slice for stuffing, make a deep incision into the pulp at the blossom end, leaving about 1 inch uncut all around the remaining sides.

→

Heat ¼ cup of the remaining olive oil in a large sauté pan or skillet pan over medium-high heat, add the eggplant slices, about three at a time, and cook, turning once or twice, until the flesh begins to soften and each side is very lightly browned, 1 to 2 minutes per side. As they are done, remove the eggplant slices to a platter. Brown the remaining eggplant slices, adding olive oil as necessary.

Stuff as much of the onion mixture as possible into each eggplant slit. Place the slices in a shallow pan with a tight-fitting lid and pour any remaining onion mixture over the top. Pour 2 cups cold water over the eggplant and cover the pan with the lid or seal tightly with foil. Bake until the eggplant is tender, about 45 minutes. Cool to room temperature, then chill for at least 2 hours or as long as 3 days. Return almost to room temperature before serving.

Serves 6 to 8 as a starter or side dish.

Creole Stewed Okra and Tomatoes

I sometimes call this old favorite, shown on page 59, Creole "ratatouille." Customarily eaten warm, I've found that the flavor improves with chilling, making it one of my favorite summertime side dishes or salad lunches.

Heat the butter in a large sauté pan or heavy pot over medium heat. Add the onion and sweet pepper and cook, stirring frequently, until the vegetables are soft but not brown, about 5 minutes. Add the okra and cook, stirring frequently, until tender, about 15 minutes.

Add the tomatoes, thyme, sugar, chili powder, and salt and peppers to taste. Cover, reduce the heat to low, and simmer until the liquid is gone and the mixture is fairly thick, about 20 minutes. Cool to room temperature, then cover and chill for as long as 2 days.

Serves 4 as a side dish or salad, or 2 as a main course.

2 tablespoons butter
1 cup chopped yellow onion
¾ cup chopped red or green sweet pepper
1 pound fresh small okra, sliced
4 or 5 medium-sized ripe tomatoes, peeled and chopped, or 1 can (28 ounces) Italian plum tomatoes, drained and chopped
1 teaspoon fresh thyme, or ¼ teaspoon dried thyme
¼ teaspoon granulated sugar
¼ teaspoon chili powder
Salt
Freshly ground black pepper
Ground cayenne pepper

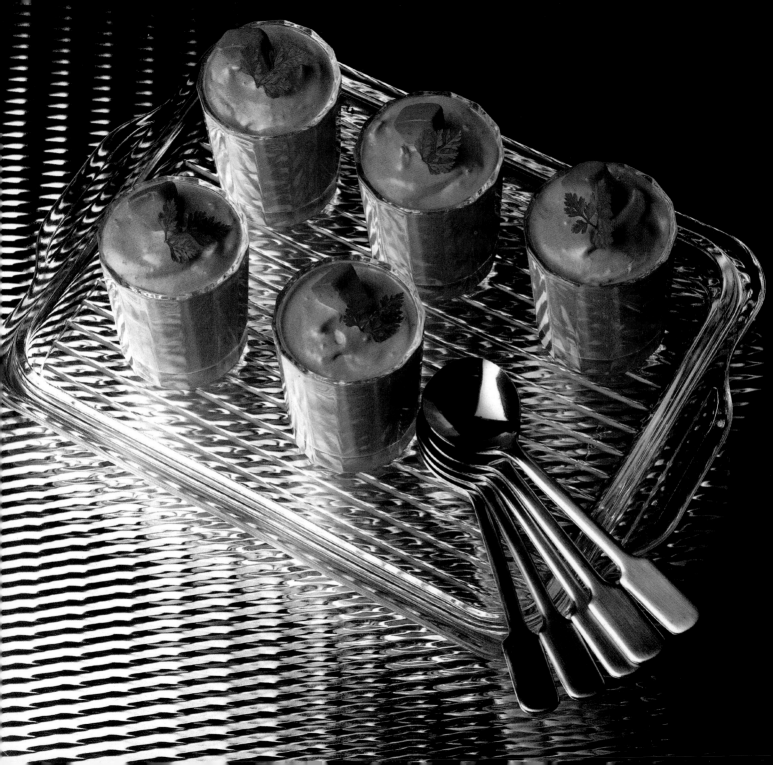

Avocado Mousse

I normally avoid passing along recipes calling for canned ingredients, but this recipe, inspired by an original one that came from England via my friend Dorothy Knecht, is so tasty and easy that I couldn't resist.

1 cup canned jellied beef consomme
2 teaspoons unflavored gelatin
3 ripe avocados
8 ounces cream cheese, at room temperature
Juice of 1 lemon
Pesticide-free edible flowers such as borage or citrus for garnish

In a small saucepan, heat ½ cup of the consomme over medium-high heat until melted. Remove from heat, sprinkle the gelatin over the top of the consomme, and let stand until the gelatin is soft, about 5 minutes. Return to heat and stir until the gelatin is dissolved, about 2 minutes. Reserve.

Pit, peel, and chop 2 of the avocados. Combine with the remaining consomme and the cream cheese in a food processor or blender and purée until smooth. Blend in the reserved gelatin mixture. Turn the mixture into demitasse cups or cocktail glasses and chill until set, at least 4 hours or as long as 24 hours. Alternatively, turn the mixture into a lightly oiled mold or bowl or into individual molds, smooth the tops, cover tightly with plastic wrap, and refrigerate until set.

Just before serving, pit, peel, and chop the remaining avocado. Dip the pieces briefly in the lemon juice to keep them from darkening. To serve, garnish the top of each mousse with chopped avocado and edible flowers; serve with demitasse spoons for eating out of the cups or glasses. If using molds, dip the lower portion of the mold into a container of hot water for several seconds, then run a thin knife blade around the inside edge of the mold. Invert onto a serving plate or individual plates, garnish, and serve.

Serves 12 as a starter.

VARIATION: Instead of the consomme, use chicken or vegetable stock and increase the amount of gelatin to 1½ tablespoons.

Layered Vegetable Terrine

5 medium-sized beets, about
1½ pounds untrimmed
1 small celery root (celeriac),
about 1 pound
3 medium-sized carrots, about
12 ounces
2 tablespoons olive oil, preferably
extra-virgin
1½ cups chopped yellow onion
¼ cup chopped shallots
1 teaspoon minced or pressed garlic,
or to taste
1½ cups milk or light cream
(half and half)
6 eggs
6 tablespoons unbleached all-purpose
flour
¾ cup freshly grated Parmesan cheese
2 tablespoons unsalted butter, melted
1 teaspoon grated lemon zest
Salt
Freshly ground white pepper
⅛ teaspoon freshly grated nutmeg,
or to taste
¼ teaspoon ground ginger, or to taste
Butter for greasing mold and lining
Chaudfroid Sauce, made with
vegetable broth (page 91;
optional)
Fresh herbs for garnish (optional)

I've used three root vegetables in writing the recipe, but similar terrines can be made with any favorite seasonal vegetables. Consider layering purées of cooked asparagus, new potatoes, and yellow squash for a pale terrine, or alternating broccoli, turnips, and pumpkin for a brighter-hued version; vary seasonings to suit individual vegetables.

The terrine can be left unadorned or covered with a layer of chaudfroid sauce and decorated with fresh herbs for a showier presentation. Serve the terrine plain or with mayonnaise, sour cream, or yogurt, each flavored to taste with minced garlic, fresh chives, or mixed herbs. Or make an uncooked salsa of chopped tomatoes.

Trim and wash the beets, being careful not to pierce the skins. Place the beets in a saucepan with warm water to cover barely. Bring to a boil, partially cover, reduce the heat to low, and simmer until very tender, about 40 minutes. (Alternatively, bake the unpeeled beets in a 300° F oven until tender, about 1 hour.) Cool, drain well, peel, measure, and reserve 2½ cups.

Peel the celery root and cut it into ½-inch cubes. Measure 2½ cups and place in a saucepan with water to cover barely. Bring to a boil and cook until very tender, about 15 minutes. Drain well and reserve.

Peel the carrots and slice them into 1-inch pieces. Measure 2½ cups and place in a steamer basket over boiling water, cover the pot, and steam until very tender, about 15 minutes; reserve.

Heat the olive oil in a sauté pan or skillet, add the onion and shallots and cook, stirring frequently, until very soft and golden, about 8 minutes. Stir in the garlic and cook 1 minute. Remove from heat.

Place the beets in a food processor or blender with about one-third of the onion mixture and ½ cup of the milk or light cream; purée until smooth. Blend in 2 eggs, 2 tablespoons of the flour, ¼ cup of the cheese, the melted butter, lemon zest, and salt and pepper to taste. Transfer to a bowl, cover, and refrigerate until very cold, preferably overnight.

→

Place the celery root in a food processor or blender with half of the remaining onion mixture and ½ cup of the remaining milk or light cream; purée until smooth. Blend in 2 eggs, 2 tablespoons of the remaining flour, ¼ cup of the cheese, the nutmeg, and salt and pepper to taste. Transfer to a bowl, cover, and refrigerate until very cold, preferably overnight.

Place the carrots in a food processor or blender with the remaining onion mixture and the remaining ½ cup milk or light cream; purée until smooth. Blend in the remaining 2 eggs, the remaining 2 tablespoons of flour, the remaining cheese, the ginger, and salt and pepper to taste. Transfer to a bowl, cover, and refrigerate until very cold, preferably overnight.

Preheat the oven to 325° F.

Cut pieces of baking parchment or waxed paper to line the bottom and sides of a 2-quart enameled terrine mold or 9 by 5 by 3-inch loaf pan. Grease the mold with butter and line with the paper. Grease the lining with butter, then spread the chilled beet mixture evenly in the bottom of the pan, cover with the chilled celery root mixture, and top with the chilled carrot mixture. Cover tightly with foil. Place inside a baking pan and add enough hot water to come halfway up the sides of the loaf pan. Bake until the center of the terrine feels set when touched with a finger, the edges have just begun to pull slightly away from the sides of the pan, and a wooden skewer tests clean when inserted in the middle of the terrine, 1½ to 2½ hours; times vary according to moisture content of the vegetables. Remove from the oven, uncover, and let stand until room temperature, then wrap tightly in plastic wrap and refrigerate overnight.

To unmold, run a knife around the edges of the terrine, cover with a plate, and invert. Remove the pan and carefully peel off the waxed paper or parchment. When using chaudfroid sauce, place the terrine on a wire rack and cover smoothly with the sauce. Refrigerate uncovered until set. Wrap in plastic wrap and chill until serving time.

To serve, return the terrine almost to room temperature, then cut into ¾-inch slices.

Serves 12 as a first course.

fish & shellfish

Sliced Raw Fish, Japanese Style
(Sashimi)

Elegant, simple, and delicious *sashimi* makes a wonderful appetizer platter for a party, a sit-down first course, or a complete light lunch or warm weather supper. It is imperative to use absolutely fresh fish and a very sharp knife. In the photo I've combined both yellowtail and red albacore tuna, cuttlefish, and octopus.

Quickly rinse the fish under cold running water and pat dry with paper toweling. Wrap tightly in plastic wrap and chill for 2 or 3 hours.

Using a fine blade, shred the daikon into a bowl of cold water and let stand until crisp, about 30 minutes. Drain well just before serving.

Mix the *wasabi* with a little water to form a thick paste; reserve.

Using a very sharp knife, slice the fish into pieces that are 2 inches long by 1 inch wide, then cut across the grain into slices ¼ inch thick, or cut into bite-sized cubes or diamond shapes. Serve immediately.

To serve, arrange the sliced fish on a platter or individual plates and garnish with the shredded daikon. Add a dollop of *wasabi*. Provide each person with a small dipping bowl of soy sauce. To eat, mix wasabi to taste with the soy sauce and use chopsticks to dip the sashimi into the sauce.

Serves 6 as a starter, or 3 or 4 as a main course.

2 pounds fresh tuna, sea bass,
    or other firm fish fillet, skinned
1 large daikon (Japanese white
    radish), peeled, for garnish
1 tablespoon *wasabi* (Japanese
    horseradish powder), or to taste
Soy sauce for dipping

Lobster with Vanilla Mayonnaise

4 1½-pound live North Atlantic
    lobsters
Salt

VANILLA MAYONNAISE
½ vanilla bean, chopped, or 2
    teaspoons vanilla extract
1 whole egg, at room temperature
1 egg yolk, at room temperature
1 teaspoon Dijon-style mustard
3 tablespoons champagne vinegar or
    freshly squeezed lemon juice
1½ cups safflower or other
    vegetable oil
Salt
Freshly ground white pepper

Whole fresh chives or watercress
    sprigs for garnish

The luxurious flavors of lobster and vanilla combine for an unexpected change. You may choose to purchase two pounds cooked lobster meat instead of cooking your own. For a lighter sauce, combine the chopped vanilla with crème fraîche.

Bring a large stockpot of water to boil over high heat. Add a generous sprinkle of salt. When the water returns to a boil, drop the lobsters head first into the water. Cook until bright red, 8 to 10 minutes. Remove the lobsters, drain, cool to room temperature, then chill for at least 1 hour or as long as overnight. Remove the claws, crack, drain out liquid, and reserve. Remove the tail and discard the vein that runs along the back; discard the bodies, reserving any bright coral-colored roe that may be found in female lobsters.

To make the mayonnaise, place the vanilla bean, if using, in a food processor or blender and grind as fine as possible. Add the egg, egg yolk, mustard, vinegar or lemon juice, and blend for about 30 seconds. Add the vanilla extract if using. With the motor running, add the oil in a slow, steady stream. When the mayonnaise thickens, turn the motor off. With a rubber or plastic spatula, scrape any oil clinging to the container and mix gently into the mayonnaise. Add salt and pepper to taste. Refrigerate for at least 1 hour to blend flavors. Mayonnaise may be refrigerated in an airtight container for up to 5 days; stir to reblend if necessary.

To serve, remove the lobster meat from each tail, reserving the shell. Slice the meat into ½-inch-thick medallions and reassemble each in the shell on individual plates. Add the claws and garnish with the chives or watercress. Add a dollop of the mayonnaise and sprinkle with any reserved roe.

Serves 4 as a main course.

Mixed Seafood Salad *(Fruits de Mer)*

As in the countless versions of "fruits of the sea" that appear throughout Mediterranean countries, use a variety of whatever seafood is locally available.

Using a long-pronged fork, rotate the peppers over an open flame (or slip them under a broiler and turn frequently) until completely charred on all sides. Place the peppers in a loosely closed paper bag until cool, about 15 minutes. Remove from the bag and rub off blackened skin with fingertips. Cut peppers in half lengthwise, remove and discard stems, seeds, and veins, and cut into long strips ½ inch wide. Reserve.

Combine the olive oil, lemon juice, garlic, basil or parsley, and salt and pepper to taste in a large bowl and whisk to blend. Add the seafood and toss to coat thoroughly. Cover with plastic wrap and marinate from 1 to 2 hours, or refrigerate for as long as overnight. Return to room temperature before serving.

To serve, arrange the seafood, reserved pepper strips, avocado slices, and olives if using, on a platter or individual plates. Drizzle with the marinade and garnish with the lemon or lime.

Serves 6 to 8 as a first course or salad, or 4 as a main course.

2 red sweet peppers
¾ cup olive oil, preferably
    extra-virgin
½ cup freshly squeezed lemon juice
3 or 4 garlic cloves, minced or pressed
2 tablespoons chopped fresh basil
    or parsley
Salt
Freshly ground black pepper
1 pound small shrimp, boiled
    (page 30), peeled, and deveined
1 pound squid, cleaned, cooked,
    and cut (page 28)
½ pound scallops, cooked in boiling
    water for 2 or 3 minutes
12 mussels or clams, cleaned and
    steamed until shells open
2 avocados, pitted, peeled, and sliced
About ½ cup Niçoise or other
    oil-cured olives (optional)
Lemon or lime slices or wedges
    for garnish

Spicy Shrimp with Oranges and Mint

This fire and ice combination was inspired by Southeast Asian cookery. Fish sauce is available in markets that specialize in Southeast Asian ingredients and some supermarkets. If you can't find it, substitute about half as much soy sauce.

Cook the shrimp according to directions on page 30. Cool, then shell and devein, leaving tails on, if desired.

Peel the oranges. With a small sharp knife, remove all white pith and cut into segments between the membranes, discarding any seeds.

In a bowl, combine the orange juice, lime juice, fish sauce, garlic, chili pepper, and salt to taste. Add the shrimp and oranges and toss well. Cover and chill for at least 1 hour and up to 4 hours. Just before serving, add the mint leaves.

Serves 4 as a salad or first course, or 2 as a main course.

1 pound large shrimp
5 medium-sized oranges
3 tablespoons freshly squeezed
   orange juice
2 tablespoons freshly squeezed
   lime juice
2 teaspoons fish sauce
3 or 4 garlic cloves, minced or pressed
½ teaspoon minced fresh red chili
   pepper or dried chili flakes, more
   or less according to taste
Salt
1 cup fresh small whole mint leaves,
   or ½ cup chopped fresh mint

Marinated Squid

4 pounds whole fresh squid, or 3
    pounds fresh or thawed frozen
    cleaned squid
Salt
¼ cup freshly squeezed lemon juice
1 cup finely chopped red onion
¾ cup finely chopped sweet fennel
    or celery
3 or 4 garlic cloves, minced or pressed
½ cup minced parsley
¼ cup chopped fresh basil (optional)
1 tablespoon minced fresh oregano,
    or 1 teaspoon dried oregano
¾ cup olive oil
¼ cup white wine vinegar
Freshly ground black pepper
6 medium-sized ripe tomatoes
    (optional)

Whether you call it calamari or squid, the marinated mollusc makes a wonderful salad or first course.

To clean the squid, hold under cold running water and pull off the speckled membrane that covers the sac or hood, then gently pull to separate the sac from the tentacles. Pull out and discard the shell or sword and any remaining contents from inside the sac. Rinse the inside of the sac, pat dry, and set aside. Slice the tentacles portion just above the eyes and discard everything except the tentacles. Squeeze out and discard the hard beak or mouth found at the base of the tentacles.

Bring 2 pots of water to a boil over high heat, add 1 tablespoon salt and 1 tablespoon lemon juice to each pot. Drop the squid tentacles into one pot and the sacs in the other; this keeps the bodies white while the tentacles turn purplish. Cook until the squid is tender, about 20 minutes. Drain well. Slice the sacs horizontally into rings ½ inch wide. If the tentacles are large, cut into small clusters.

In a bowl, combine the onion, fennel or celery, garlic, parsley, basil, oregano, olive oil, vinegar, remaining 2 tablespoons of lemon juice, and salt and pepper to taste. Whisk to blend, then toss with the cooked squid. Cover tightly and refrigerate at least 24 hours and as long as 2 days, stirring from time to time. Drain the marinade before serving.

To serve in tomato shells, cut off the stem ends, then cut a cavity with a small serrated knife and remove the pulp and seeds with a spoon or melon ball scoop. Place upside down on a wire rack to drain, then spoon in the squid.

Serves 6 to 8 as a starter or salad.

Boiled Crawfish or Shrimp

20 pounds small crawfish, or 6 pounds medium-sized shrimp, (about 20 per pound)
1 cup commercial shrimp or crab boil (see note)
2 lemons, sliced
2 large onions, quartered
4 or 5 garlic cloves, smashed
2 tablespoons salt

When you don't have access to delectable fresh crawfish, crayfish, crawdaddies, or mudbuggies, depending on where you live, substitute meatier shrimp. The boiling seasonings in this recipe add plenty of flavor to the shellfish, but you may want to offer a tomato-based cocktail sauce or other favorite cold fish sauce.

To serve, mound the crawfish or shrimp in the middle of a table spread with newspapers to collect shells as shown on page 4. Or for a dressier presentation, arrange on crushed ice on individual plates.

If the shellfish are live, soak them in a large pot of cold water for 10 to 20 minutes, then rinse them thoroughly under cold running water.

In a 12-quart pot, combine 6 quarts water, the shrimp or crab boil, lemons, onions, and garlic and bring to a boil over high heat. Add the salt, cover the pot, reduce the heat to low, and simmer 20 minutes to combine the flavors.

Return the stock to a boil, drop in the shellfish in batches, and boil until they turn bright pink, about 5 minutes; return the stock to a brisk boil between each batch. Remove with a slotted spoon as soon as the crawfish or shrimp are done and rinse them in cold water to prevent further cooking. Drain well, then pack in ice or cover and refrigerate until well chilled, at least 2 hours or as long as overnight.

Serves 6 to 8 as a main course.

NOTE: With the current interest in Louisiana foods, commercial shrimp or crab boil is available in most supermarkets or fish markets. If you can't find it, combine 4 or 5 dried red chili peppers, crumbled, ¼ cup *each* coriander and mustard seeds, 2 tablespoons *each* whole allspice and dill seeds, 1 tablespoon whole cloves, and 2 or 3 bay leaves, crumbled.

Marinated Fried Fish Fillets, Venetian Style *(Sfogi in Saor)*

On the night of the Feast of the Holy Redeemer, Venetians celebrate with fireworks. This centuries-old dish is commonly a part of the meal served aboard the countless boats that fill the sea and the canals. There it's always made with firm Adriatic sole, but I enjoy it with catfish— my native Louisiana meets my soul country of Italy.

Heat the olive oil in a heavy sauté pan or skillet over medium-high heat. Add the onion, cover the pan, reduce the heat to low, and cook, stirring occasionally, until the onion is soft, about 15 minutes. Remove the cover, increase the heat to medium, and cook, stirring frequently, until the onion is golden brown and almost caramelized, about 45 minutes longer. Increase the heat to high, add the vinegar, and cook until the liquid evaporates, about 5 minutes. Remove from the heat and reserve.

Quickly rinse the fish fillets under cold running water and pat dry with paper toweling. Dredge the fillets in flour to lightly coat; shake off excess flour.

Pour vegetable oil into a skillet to a depth of ½ inch and heat over high heat until hot enough to brown a cube of bread quickly. Add the fish and fry until golden brown on all sides, about 5 minutes. As soon as pieces are done, remove with a slotted spoon to paper toweling to drain. Sprinkle with salt to taste.

Place the fish snugly in a dish, overlapping if necessary, then cover with the onion mixture. Drain the raisins, then pat dry with paper toweling and sprinkle them and the pine nuts over the top of the onion mixture. Cover tightly with plastic wrap and refrigerate overnight or up to 2 days. Return to room temperature before serving.

Serves 10 as a starter, or 6 as a main course.

3 tablespoons olive oil, preferably extra-virgin
2 cups chopped yellow onion
1½ cups white wine vinegar
1½ pounds sole or catfish fillets
Flour for dredging
Vegetable oil for frying
Salt
⅓ cup golden raisins, soaked for 30 minutes in warm water
¼ cup pine nuts, lightly toasted

Scallop and Salmon Mousses

2 tablespoons unsalted butter
2 tablespoons all-purpose flour
1½ cups homemade fish stock (page 92), or 1 cup canned chicken broth diluted with ½ cup water
12 ounces cooked scallops, coarsely chopped
Salt
Freshly ground pepper
2 envelopes (2 tablespoons) unflavored gelatin
½ cup heavy (whipping) cream, whipped
12 ounces cooked salmon fillet, coarsely chopped
4 ounces caviar

Although time-consuming, this elegant presentation is quite easy to prepare. Serve with the finest black, red, or golden caviar you can afford.

Melt the butter in a saucepan over medium heat, add the flour, and cook for about 3 minutes. Using a wire whisk, blend in 1 cup of the fish stock or diluted chicken broth and cook until sauce is smooth and thick, about 5 minutes. Reserve the sauce.

To make the scallop mousse, combine the cooked scallops with ½ cup of the reserved sauce in a food processor or blender and purée until fairly smooth. Press through a sieve into a bowl and season to taste with salt and pepper. Sprinkle 1 envelope of the gelatin over ¼ cup of the remaining fish stock or diluted chicken broth in a small saucepan and let stand until soft, about 5 minutes. Place over medium-high heat and stir until the gelatin is dissolved, about 2 minutes. Cool slightly, then stir into the scallop mixture. Divide the whipped cream in half, reserving one half for the salmon mousse. Stir 2 tablespoons of one portion of the cream into the scallop mousse to lighten the mixture, then gently fold in the remaining portion of cream with a rubber spatula. Cover and refrigerate while you make the salmon mousse.

To make the salmon mousse, prepare in the same manner as the scallop mixture, using the salmon, the remaining white sauce, gelatin, stock or broth, and whipped cream. Cover and refrigerate for about 15 minutes.

→

Turn the salmon mousse into a lightly oiled 1-quart mold or individual molds, then fill the mold or molds with the reserved scallop mousse. Shake the mold on the counter top several times to prevent any air holes between the layers. Smooth the top of the mousse. Cover tightly with plastic wrap and chill until set, at least 4 hours and as long as overnight.

To unmold, dip the mold into hot water for a few seconds, run a dull knife blade around the inside edges of the mold, place a dish over the top, and invert the mousse onto the dish. Garnish with caviar. Slice the large molded mousse to serve or present individual mousses whole.

Serves 8 to 10 as a starter, or 6 as a main course.

poultry

Spiced Poached Chicken Breasts

Food writer Elizabeth David's recipe for this Middle Eastern delicacy inspired my version, which is delicious teamed with a couscous or cracked wheat (bulgur) salad made with lots of parsley, green onion, and tomato in a lemony vinaigrette. For a richer and tastier version, use fresh or canned coconut milk for the poaching liquid.

2 teaspoons whole coriander seeds
1½ tablespoons minced peeled fresh ginger root
1 tablespoon minced or grated lemon zest (with no bitter white pith)
1 teaspoon husked cardamom seeds
¼ teaspoon ground cloves
Salt
Ground cayenne pepper
6 boned and skinned chicken breast halves
About 3 cups milk
2 eggs, beaten
Chopped pistachio nuts for garnish
Minced or grated lemon zest for garnish

Put the coriander seeds in a small skillet over medium heat, and toast the seeds, stirring or shaking the pan, until lightly toasted, about 5 minutes. Empty onto a plate to cool.

In a food processor or blender, combine the coriander seeds, ginger, lemon zest, cardamom seeds, cloves, and salt and pepper to taste. Grind finely.

Quickly rinse the chicken breasts under cold running water and pat dry with paper toweling. Sprinkle with the spice mixture, pressing it into the flesh, cover, and refrigerate for at least 2 hours or as long as overnight. Return to room temperature before cooking.

Place the chicken breasts in a skillet or wide saucepan and add enough milk to cover. Bring to a boil over medium heat and immediately reduce the heat so the liquid barely ripples. Simmer the breasts uncovered until they are done, about 12 minutes. The meat should be moist and opaque throughout; cook only to just beyond the pink stage. Remove the breasts with a slotted spoon and drain well; reserve the cooking liquid. Cool the chicken to room temperature.

Measure 2 cups of the cooking liquid into the top portion of a double boiler set over simmering water. When hot, add about ¼ cup to the beaten eggs, stirring continuously to prevent curdling. Stir this mixture back into the double boiler. Cook, stirring continuously, until thickened, about 5 minutes. Pour the sauce over the chicken breasts and chill uncovered for about 1 hour. Or cover with a bowl or other dome and chill as long as overnight. Return to room temperature before serving. To serve, garnish with pistachios and lemon zest.

Serves 6 as a main course.

Chicken in Mango Mayonnaise

5 chicken breast halves
About 3 cups homemade chicken
    stock or canned broth
1 ripe mango
1½ cups Mayonnaise (page 92), or
    good-quality commercial
    mayonnaise
1 cup green seedless grapes
5 green onions, minced
½ cup minced celery
Pesticide-free borage flowers
    for garnish

The idea for this dish was suggested by host Harvey Steinman when I appeared on San Francisco's *KCBS Kitchen* to chat about my book on chicken. English wheatmeal biscuits are the perfect accompaniment.

To poach the chicken breasts, place them in a skillet or saucepan with just enough chicken stock or water to cover. Bring to a boil over medium heat and immediately reduce the heat so the liquid barely ripples. Simmer the breasts uncovered until done, about 12 minutes. The meat should be moist throughout; cook only to just beyond the pink stage. Remove breasts with a slotted spoon and drain well. Cool to room temperature, then remove and discard skin and bones. Cut meat into bite-sized pieces; reserve.

Peel and seed the mango and place the pulp in a food processor or blender and purée until smooth. Add the mayonnaise and blend well.

In a large bowl, combine the reserved chicken with the grapes, onions, and celery, then toss with the mayonnaise to thoroughly coat. Serve immediately at room temperature or chill slightly before serving. Garnish with borage flowers.

Serves 6 to 8 as a first course, or 4 as a main course.

Duck Galantine

2 3- to 4-pound fresh ducks
9 fresh parsley sprigs
6 fresh thyme sprigs
3 bay leaves
2 medium-sized onions, quartered
2 medium-sized carrots, cut into
    2-inch pieces
2 celery ribs, cut into 2-inch pieces
Salt
Freshly ground black pepper
8 ounces boned veal
8 ounces *pancetta* (Italian spiced,
    cured pork) or bacon
1 tablespoon minced fresh sage
2 teaspoons minced fresh thyme
Grated zest of 1 orange or lemon
½ cup chopped pistachios
3 tablespoons green peppercorns
1½ ounces fresh or preserved black
    truffles, diced
2 tablespoons vegetable oil
Aspic (page 90), made with stock
    from poaching the galantine
Green peppercorns for garnish

Aptly adapted from *galant*, meaning gentlemanly, this elegant form of pâté originally kept painstakingly true to the shape of the animal from which it was made. Most charcuterie cooks today fashion the stuffed boned meat into a roll that's not only easier to prepare but distributes the meat and forcemeat filling more evenly. Chicken, turkey, or other fowl can be prepared in the same way.

Upon completion, the galantine may be served as is or covered with chaudfroid sauce (page 91) made from the stock used in poaching the galantine, then decorated for a more elegant presentation.

Clean, wash, and singe the ducks to remove all pinfeathers. Position each duck breast-side up on a cutting surface and cut off the neck, the pope's nose, the wings at the joint, and the lower legs at the knee joint. Turn the ducks over breast-side down and cut through the skin from the neck to the tail on both sides of the backbone. Be careful from now on not to cut through the skin of the ducks at any point. Using your fingers inside the skin, locate the thigh joints. Cut through each with a sharp knife held in one hand while you turn the leg with the other hand. Locate and cut the wing joints in the same way.

With a sharp knife held with the blade toward the carcass from inside the bird, cut along each side of the rib cage to separate the meat from the bones. Carefully cut out the breastbone while holding the bone away from the skin. Reserve the carcass and breastbone. With a small sharp knife, cut through the ligaments around the knuckle of each leg bone, then scrape the meat off the bone. Hold the meat in place as you pull the bone through from the inside. Reserve the bones. Remove and reserve the wing bones in the same way. Carefully cut or pull out all ligaments in the leg and wing area; use a small pair of kitchen pliers if necessary.

→

Wrap 3 parsley sprigs, 2 thyme sprigs, and 1 bay leaf in cheesecloth and tie with cotton string. Make 2 more identical *bouquets garni* and reserve.

Chop the reserved bones. Place half of them in a stockpot, add 1 *bouquet garni* and cover the bones with cold water. Bring to a boil over high heat, then reduce the heat to low and simmer to make a light broth, about 1 hour. Strain and reserve.

Place the remaining bones in a second stockpot, add a *bouquet garni*, the onions, carrots, celery, and salt and pepper to taste. Cover with water and bring to a boil over high heat, then reduce the heat to low and simmer to make a stock, about 1 to 2 hours. Strain the stock through a fine wire sieve, season with additional salt and pepper as needed, and cook over high heat until reduced to about ⅓ cup, about 45 minutes. Reserve.

Select the duck with the best skin intact, spread the meat out evenly, and cut off any skin that does not have meat attached. Wrap in plastic wrap and refrigerate until needed. Remove, wrap, and refrigerate the breasts from the second duck. Discard the skin from the second duck and cut the remaining meat into ½-inch cubes. Coarsely chop the veal and *pancetta* or bacon. Combine the duck meat, veal, and *pancetta* or bacon in a bowl and sprinkle with salt to taste, the minced sage, thyme, and orange or lemon zest. Mix well, cover tightly, and refrigerate until very cold, about 2 hours. Chill the bowl of a food processor as well.

Place the cold meat mixture in the chilled bowl and process until smooth and light. Push the mixture through a sieve to remove any bits of ligament or skin that remain. Stir in 2½ tablespoons of the thickened duck stock. Fold in the pistachios, peppercorns, and truffles; reserve.

Remove the duck breasts from the refrigerator and season to taste with salt and pepper. Heat the vegetable oil in a sauté pan or skillet over high heat, add the breasts, and cook briefly on all sides to seal and lightly brown, about 2 minutes total. Remove the duck breasts to paper toweling to drain.

Spread out the reserved whole duck on a flat surface and spread about half of the chilled forcemeat across the middle of the duck; the forcemeat should go all the way across from side to side but leave about 4 inches of meat exposed at both the tail and neck ends. Trim the ends from the sautéed breasts and place the breasts end to end on top of the forcemeat. Brush with the remaining thickened duck stock, then cover with the remaining forcemeat. Fold the tail end over the forcemeat, then fold the neck end over. Shape the duck into an even roll, pressing to seal all joints and eliminate air pockets.

Place the roll on several layers of cheesecloth or a clean cloth dish towel. Wrap the roll firmly but not too tightly in the cloth, then tie each end securely with cotton string. Tie with string at 1-inch intervals along the roll. Weigh the galantine on a kitchen scale.

Place the galantine in a roasting pan or other pot and pour in enough of the reserved strained broth to cover. Remove the galantine and bring the broth to a simmer over medium heat. Gently lower the galantine into the hot broth and simmer until done, about 20 minutes per pound. Test by inserting a large needle in the center; it should meet little resistance. Remove the pot from the heat. Cover the galantine with a clean board and a 3- or 4-pound weight, such as canned food, to keep it immersed in the broth. Refrigerate for 24 hours.

Remove the galantine from the broth. Discard any fat from the surface of the broth and reserve it to prepare the aspic.

Untie the galantine, rinse under warm running water to remove all fat from the surface, and pat dry with paper toweling.

→

Prepare the aspic as directed on page 90. Pour half of it into a bowl, cover, and refrigerate until hard enough for chopping. When the remaining aspic chills to the consistency of honey, place the galantine on a wire rack and coat with aspic. Refrigerate uncovered until the aspic sets up, about 15 minutes. Add decorations and additional aspic as desired. Once the final coatings have set, wrap loosely in plastic wrap or cover with a foil tent and refrigerate.

To serve, slice the galantine into ½-inch-thick slices and garnish with green peppercorns and chopped aspic.

Serves 10 as a first course, or 4 to 6 as a main course.

Rabbit and Prune Compote

San Francisco gourmet partygiver Stephen Suzman once served this interpretation of a Paula Wolfert version of an old French recipe at a luxurious picnic spread on lush grass in front of a rose-entwined gazebo. The original recipe calls for mature wild or domestic rabbit, but most of us only have access to the young fryer rabbits sold in supermarkets.

Stephen and I prefer the rabbit without the traditional aspic coating. If you wish to add aspic, see page 90. In either case, be sure to start the dish three days before serving.

Vary the garnish according to the season. Serve with your choice of toasted brioche slices, buttered whole-grain bread, endive spears, celery sticks, firm Fuyu persimmon slices, or buttery pear slices tossed in a little lemon juice to keep them from turning dark.

Have the butcher bone the rabbit, reserving the bones and meat separately. Or use a sharp knife to cut and scrape the meat from the bones; reserve each.

In a nonreactive bowl, combine the wine, onions, carrot, olive oil, shallots, and garlic. Tie the rabbit meat loosely in cheesecloth, add it to the marinade, and toss to coat thoroughly. Cover and refrigerate overnight, shaking or stirring occasionally.

Blanch the *pancetta* or salt pork in boiling water for about 4 minutes, then cool and chop.

Heat the vegetable oil in a dutch oven or large, ovenproof casserole over medium-high heat, add the *pancetta* or salt pork, and sauté until lightly browned. Using a slotted spoon, remove the *pancetta* to drain on paper toweling; do not rinse pot.

→

1 4-pound mature rabbit,
    or 2 young rabbits (about 4
    pounds total), cut up
2 cups dry white wine
3 medium-sized yellow onions,
    thinly sliced
½ cup sliced carrot
⅔ cup olive oil, preferably
    extra-virgin
2 shallots, chopped
1 or 2 garlic cloves, chopped
5 ounces *pancetta* (Italian spiced,
    cured pork) or lean salt pork
2½ teaspoons vegetable oil
2 teaspoons Dijon-style mustard
4 cups unsalted chicken stock or
    canned low-sodium broth
4 fresh parsley sprigs
2 fresh thyme sprigs, or ½ teaspoon
    dried thyme
1 fresh rosemary sprig, or ¼
    teaspoon dried rosemary
1 cup Cognac
18 pitted prunes
18 walnut halves, lightly toasted
¾ cup heavy (whipping) cream
Freshly squeezed lemon juice
Salt
Freshly ground black pepper
Pesticide-free edible flowers such as
    acacia or small violas, or
    persimmon or other colorful
    autumn leaves for garnish

Remove the rabbit meat from the marinade, unwrap, and reserve. Strain the marinade through a wire sieve into a bowl; reserve. Add the onion mixture to the pot with the *pancetta* drippings, reduce the heat to low, and cook, stirring frequently, until the onion mixture is almost caramelized, about 45 minutes. Stir in the mustard and transfer to a bowl; do not rinse pot.

Preheat the oven to 300° F.

Place the pot over medium-high heat and scrape the pan bottom with a wooden spoon to loosen browned bits. Add the strained marinade and the stock and bring to a boil. Using cotton string, tie the onion mixture and the herbs in cheesecloth and add to the liquid. Loosely tie the reserved rabbit bones in several layers of cheesecloth and add to the liquid. Add the reserved rabbit meat and *pancetta* or salt pork. Stir to blend well, cover with a lid or foil, and place in the oven. Cook, frequently skimming off any surface foam, until the meat is very tender, about 4 hours. Remove from the oven and cool to room temperature. Strain the liquid into a bowl and transfer the rabbit to a separate bowl, discarding the bags of onion and bones. Cover both the rabbit and the liquid tightly with plastic wrap and refrigerate for several hours or as long as overnight.

Heat the Cognac in a small saucepan and pour over prunes in a bowl. Let stand until the prunes are soft and plumped, about 20 minutes, then stuff each prune with a walnut half; reserve.

Remove and discard the accumulated fat from the top of the chilled liquid. Pour the liquid in a saucepan over medium heat and cook, skimming frequently, until reduced by half, about 15 minutes. Stir in the cream and adjust the heat so the liquid cooks at a brisk simmer without boiling until reduced by half, about 25 minutes. Season the sauce to taste with lemon juice, salt, and pepper.

Meanwhile, break up the rabbit mixture with a fork and place half in a plain 1½-quart mold or crock. Add a layer of the stuffed prunes, reserving some for garnish. Cover with the remaining rabbit mixture and pour the hot liquid over the top. Cool, then cover with plastic wrap and refrigerate for at least 24 hours or as long as 2 days.

To serve, unmold the compote onto a platter and garnish with the remaining prunes and the flowers or leaves.

Serves 8 to 12 as a first course, or 6 as a main course.

Sliced Raw Beef, Italian Style (*Carpaccio*)

2 pounds boned beef fillet or other tender cut, trimmed of all fat

MUSTARD SAUCE
1 cup Mayonnaise (page 92), or good-quality commercial mayonnaise
1 tablespoon Worcestershire sauce
1 teaspoon dry mustard
½ teaspoon Tabasco sauce
⅓ cup flavorful homemade beef stock (page 92) or canned broth
2 teaspoons freshly squeezed lemon juice
Red, white, and pink peppercorns, crushed, for garnish (optional)

Carpaccio is traditionally eaten as a first course with small pieces of Parmesan cheese, but with a green salad and some crusty bread, it makes a fine summer lunch. Or serve a platter of the tender beef as part of a buffet. Italian cooks disagree about the sauce—some advocate only olive oil and lemon juice, and others would object to the use of mustard in the mayonnaise-based sauce that follows; I think the mustard goes well with the beef.

Quickly rinse the beef under running cold water and pat dry with paper toweling. Wrap in freezer wrap and place in the freezer until the meat is very cold but not frozen through, about 2 hours.

To make the sauce, combine the mayonnaise, Worcestershire, mustard, Tabasco, stock or broth, and lemon juice in a small bowl and whisk with a wire whisk or stir with a wooden spoon until smooth. Cover and refrigerate until needed.

Using an electric knife or electric slicer, slice the beef as thinly as possible. (Or have the butcher slice the meat.) Arrange on a plate and smear with some of the sauce if desired. Garnish with peppercorns if using and serve with the remaining sauce.

Serves 8 as a starter, or 4 as a light main dish.

Beef Salad, Thai Style

In Thailand this dish is usually served as a snack. Try it as a tasty first course, light lunch or supper, or an unusual party platter. Fish sauce and lemon grass are available at markets that specialize in Southeast Asian foods. If you can't locate them, I've listed adequate substitutes.

Grill, broil, or roast the beef until medium rare. Cool, then slice into half-inch-wide strips about 2 inches long. Reserve.

In a large bowl, combine the lime or lemon juice, fish or soy sauce, sugar, chili peppers, garlic, minced cilantro, mint, and lemon grass or zest. Whisk to blend well, then add the reserved beef and toss to coat thoroughly.

Arrange the lettuce or other greens on a platter or individual plates. Spoon on the beef and top with the onion rings and tomato slices. Garnish with the bean sprouts, cilantro leaves, lime slices, and nasturtiums if using.

Serves 8 as a first course, or 4 or 5 as a main course.

2 pounds boneless beef tenderloin or other tender cut, trimmed of all fat
½ cup freshly squeezed lime or lemon juice
¼ cup fish sauce, or 2 tablespoons soy sauce
2 tablespoons granulated sugar
2 tablespoons minced fresh red chili peppers, or ½ tablespoon crushed dried chili pepper
6 garlic cloves, minced or pressed
3 or 4 fresh cilantro (coriander) stalks, including roots, minced
¼ cup chopped fresh mint leaves
1 stalk fresh lemon grass, tender bottom only, minced, or 2 teaspoons minced lemon zest
About 4 cups tender lettuce or other salad greens
1 red onion, thinly sliced and separated into rings
1 large ripe yellow or red tomato, sliced
Fresh bean sprouts for garnish
Fresh cilantro (coriander) for garnish
Lime slices for garnish
Pesticide-free nasturtiums for garnish (optional)

Wild Rice and Beef in Red Pepper Dressing

4 cups light homemade beef stock
    (page 92), or 2 cups canned beef
    broth diluted with 2 cups water
1 cup wild rice
2 pounds tenderloin or other tender
    beef cut
1 red sweet pepper
1 cup Mayonnaise (page 92), or
    good-quality commercial
    mayonnaise
1 tablespoon freshly squeezed lemon
    juice
1 teaspoon minced or pressed garlic
5 or 6 green onions, including some
    of the green tops, finely chopped
Salt
Freshly ground black pepper
2 large ripe papayas (optional)
Red sweet pepper strips for garnish

Lake Tahoe caterer Barbara Grant featured a similar salad in her charming outdoor summer Gardens restaurant.

To cook the rice, bring the stock (or broth and water) to a boil in a wide-bottomed saucepan, stir in the rice, and return to a boil. Reduce the heat to very low, cover, and simmer until the grains pop open, about 45 minutes. Remove from heat, drain off any excess water; cover the pot with paper toweling, replace lid, and let stand until dry, about 5 minutes. Fluff the grains with a fork. Reserve.

Grill or roast the beef until done to your taste, cool, then slice into thin strips; reserve.

Using a long-pronged fork, rotate the sweet pepper over an open flame (or slip under a broiler and turn frequently) until completely charred on all sides. Place the pepper in a loosely closed paper bag until cool, about 15 minutes. Remove from the bag and rub off blackened skin with fingertips. Cut pepper in half lengthwise, remove and discard stem, seeds, and veins. Coarsely chop the pepper and transfer to a food processor or blender. Add the mayonnaise, lemon juice, and garlic and purée until smooth.

In a large bowl, combine the rice, beef, green onions, red pepper mayonnaise, and salt and pepper to taste. Serve at room temperature or refrigerate as long as overnight. Return to room temperature before serving.

To serve in papaya shells, peel, halve, and seed the papayas and stuff with the rice mixture. Garnish with red pepper strips.

Serves 4 as a main dish.

Molded Jellied Beef, Creole Style
(Daube Glacé)

2 tablespoons vegetable oil
1 4- to 5-pound bottom round or
   shoulder beef roast, trimmed of
   excess fat
2 medium-sized yellow onions,
   coarsely chopped
3 carrots, coarsely chopped
4 or 5 garlic cloves, coarsely chopped
1 tablespoon minced fresh parsley
5 whole cloves
1 tablespoon fresh thyme, or
   1 teaspoon dried thyme
Salt
Freshly ground black pepper
½ cup red wine
1 to 2 quarts homemade beef stock
   (page 92), or canned broth,
   brought to a simmer
3 tablespoons (3 envelopes)
   unflavored gelatin
3 carrots, peeled and cut into very
   small dice
3 tablespoons minced fresh parsley
3 teaspoons minced or pressed garlic
1 tablespoon Worcestershire sauce
1 teaspoon ground cayenne pepper,
   or to taste
Lemon slices for garnish
Shredded lettuce for garnish

New Orleans' most famous cold meat preparation features shreds of tender braised beef suspended in a spicy brown meat jelly. Although a few Creole cooks continue to make the jelly from bones and pigs' feet, most now opt for this more convenient method. Purists also stud the beef with pork fat and brown the meat in lard before cooking; I've cut down on the fats while still producing flavorful meat.

French bread and butter are the traditional accompaniments. In the photograph, the beef is served with Creole Stewed Okra and Tomatoes (page 13).

Heat the vegetable oil in a large stockpot or dutch oven over high heat, add the meat, and turn to brown well on all sides. Remove the meat and add the onions, chopped carrots, coarsely chopped garlic, parsley, cloves, thyme, and salt and black pepper to taste. Cook until the vegetables are soft and golden, 10 to 15 minutes. Return the meat to the pot and add the wine and just enough of the simmering stock to barely cover the beef. Cover the pot, reduce the heat to low, and simmer until the beef is very tender but not falling apart, about 3 hours. Remove from heat and cool the beef in the stock.

Remove the meat from the stock and shred or cut it into strips that are about ¼ inch wide and 2 inches long; reserve. Strain the stock into a bowl through several layers of cheesecloth; reserve.

Sprinkle the gelatin into 1 cup cold water in a saucepan and let stand until softened, about 5 minutes. Place over medium-high heat and stir until the gelatin is dissolved, about 2 minutes; reserve.

In a large bowl, combine the shredded beef with 1½ quarts of the reserved stock, the dissolved gelatin, diced carrots, minced parsley, minced garlic, Worcestershire, cayenne pepper, and salt to taste; mix well.

→

Dip the lemon slices into the mixture to coat with liquid, then arrange them on the bottom of a loaf pan 9 x 5 x 3 inches or a 2-quart mold. Pour in the beef mixture. Cover tightly with plastic wrap and chill for at least 12 hours and as long as 2 days.

Before unmolding, scrape off any congealed fat that has formed on top. Run a thin knife blade around the inside of the pan or mold and briefly dip the bottom of the mold in a container of hot water for a few seconds to loosen the *daube glacé*. Cover with a serving platter, invert, and tap the pan all around to unmold the *daube glacé*. Refrigerate until ready to serve. Surround with the shredded lettuce just before serving.

To serve, divide into inch-thick slices; don't expect neat slices.

Serves 8 as a first course, or 4 as a main course.

Stuffed Veal Breast
(Petto di Vitello Ripieno)

Genoa is home of this Italian specialty that's usually stuffed with ground meats, bread crumbs, or spinach. Broccoli stuffing is a delectable alternative.

Rinse the veal under cold running water and pat dry with paper toweling. Position the veal ribs down on a cutting surface. Using a sharp knife, insert the blade between the meat and the bones. Work as closely as possible to the bones and cut the meat away, leaving in one piece. Reserve the bones. If you wish, have the butcher bone the veal; be sure to bring home the bones.

Lay the veal flat and cut a slit or pocket by slicing the meat horizontally from one end, leaving three sides attached. Reserve.

Place the veal bones in a stockpot, add enough water to cover, and bring to a boil over medium-high heat. Remove any scum that rises to the surface. Add the onions, leeks, celery, carrots, parsley, rosemary, bay leaves, peppercorns, and salt to taste. Return to a boil, reduce the heat to low, cover, and simmer until the vegetables are very tender and the stock is flavorful, about 2 to 3 hours, skimming as necessary. Strain the stock, discarding bones and vegetables.

To make the stuffing, heat the olive oil in a sauté pan or skillet over medium-high heat, add the broccoli and garlic, and sauté until the broccoli is bright green and softened, about 5 minutes. Transfer to a large bowl and add the parsley, bread crumbs, *prosciutto* or ham, cheese, eggs, and salt and pepper to taste; mix well.

→

1 5- to 6-pound breast of veal
2 large onions, quartered
2 leeks, split lengthwise and washed (optional)
2 celery stalks, cut into 2-inch pieces
3 carrots, cut into 2-inch pieces
4 fresh parsley sprigs, preferably flat-leaf Italian type
2 sprigs fresh rosemary, or 1 teaspoon dried rosemary
2 bay leaves
1 teaspoon black peppercorns
Salt
2 tablespoons olive oil
2 pounds broccoli, florets and tender upper half of stalks only, very finely chopped, preferably in a food processor
1 tablespoon minced or pressed garlic
½ cup minced fresh parsley, preferably flat-leaf Italian type
1 cup fresh bread crumbs, from French bread
5 ounces *prosciutto* or other flavorful ham, finely chopped
1 cup freshly grated Parmesan cheese
3 eggs, lightly beaten
Freshly ground black pepper
5 hardcooked eggs

Insert half of the stuffing into the veal breast pocket. Trim the rounded ends off the hard-cooked eggs until yolk shows at each end, then line them up end to end down the center of the stuffing. Cover with the remaining stuffing. Sew up the pocket opening with heavy cotton thread. Tie the meat lengthwise with cotton string, then tie crosswise in several places. Place it in a large pan and pour in enough veal stock to cover by 2 or 3 inches, adding water if necessary. Bring to a boil over medium-high heat, reduce the heat to low, and simmer uncovered for 1 hour. Cover the pot and simmer until the meat tests tender when pierced with a wooden skewer, about 1 hour longer. Remove the pot from the heat and let the veal cool in the stock.

Transfer the cooled veal to a shallow pan. Boil the stock over high heat until it is reduced by half, then strain and reserve for making aspic or soup. Wrap the veal in plastic wrap or a clean cloth, cover with a clean board, place a heavy weight on top, and refrigerate for several hours or as long as overnight.

To serve, unwrap the veal, remove the thread, and carve into slices ½ inch thick.

Serves 6 to 8 as a main dish.

Poached Veal in Tuna Sauce
(Vitello Tonnato)

POACHED VEAL
2½ pounds lean boned veal top round
1 medium-sized onion, sliced
1 medium-sized carrot, cut into
    2-inch pieces
1 celery stalk, cut into 2-inch pieces
3 fresh parsley sprigs
2 bay leaves
1 teaspoon whole white peppercorns
Dry white wine for poaching
    (optional)

TUNA SAUCE
1 can (7 ounces) tuna fish packed in
    oil, preferably olive oil
5 or 6 flat anchovy fillets packed in
    oil, rinsed and patted dry
3 to 4 tablespoons drained capers
1 cup virgin olive oil
¼ cup freshly squeezed lemon juice
    or white wine vinegar
1½ cups Mayonnaise (page 92), or
    good-quality commercial
    mayonnaise
Salt
Freshly ground white pepper

Thin lemon slices for garnish
Capers for garnish
Fresh parsley leaflets, preferably
    flat-leaf Italian type, for garnish

A book on chilled cuisine would be incomplete without this Italian pairing of poached veal with tuna sauce. Plan to make it the day before serving to allow time for the flavors to blend.

Rinse the veal under running cold water and pat dry with paper toweling. Roll it tightly and tie with cotton string at 1-inch intervals. Place it in a pot in which it just fits comfortably. Add the onion, carrot, celery, parsley, bay leaves, and peppercorns. Add just enough water, wine, or a combination of both to cover. Remove the veal. Bring the liquid to a boil over medium heat, add the veal, and return to a boil, then cover the pot, reduce the heat to low, and simmer until the meat tests very tender when pierced with a skewer or fork, about 2 hours. Remove the pot from the heat and let the veal cool in the liquid.

To make the sauce, combine the tuna, anchovies, capers, olive oil, and lemon juice or vinegar in a food processor or blender and blend until smooth. Put the mayonnaise in a mixing bowl and fold the tuna mixture into it. Add salt and pepper to taste.

Remove the strings from the cooled veal and slice it into ¼-inch-thick slices.

Spread a thin layer of the tuna sauce on a platter. Arrange a layer of sliced veal over the sauce, then cover with more sauce. Continue layering until the veal and sauce are used, ending with a layer of sauce. Cover tightly with plastic wrap and refrigerate at least overnight or for up to 3 days.

Remove from the refrigerator a few minutes before serving. Garnish with lemon slices, capers, and parsley.

Serves 8 to 10 as a starter, or 6 as a main course.

VARIATIONS: Use the sauce over cold poached chicken breasts, pork loin, or fish fillets.

Veal and Pork Terrine

Serve this easy-to-make, country-style terrine right from its baking dish with good crusty bread and your favorite mustard.

In a large bowl, combine the veal, pork, bacon, garlic, juniper berries, thyme, sage, marjoram, crushed bay leaf, nutmeg, and salt and pepper to taste. Stir in the wine, cover tightly with plastic wrap, and refrigerate overnight.

Working in small batches, place the meat mixture in a food processor and run until coarsely chopped. Transfer the mixture to a large bowl, add the eggs, and beat with a wooden spoon or electric mixer until well blended, about 8 minutes.

Preheat the oven to 325° F.

Line a 5- or 6-cup earthenware terrine with the sliced fat, fill with the meat mixture, and smooth the top. Garnish with juniper berries, bay leaves, and herb sprigs. Cut a piece of baking parchment to fit snugly inside the terrine and cover the top of the garnished meat. Cover with a lid or foil and place the dish in a large deep pan. Add enough hot water to come halfway up the sides of the terrine and bake until done throughout and set, 1 to 1½ hours. Remove from the heat and cool to room temperature.

If desired, prepare the aspic as described on page 90 and pour over the top of the cooled terrine. Cover tightly with plastic wrap and refrigerate overnight.

Serves 8 to 10 as a starter, or 5 or 6 as a main course.

1 pound boned veal, with some fat
1 pound boned pork, with some fat
1 pound thick-sliced bacon, coarsely chopped
3 garlic cloves, minced or pressed
1 tablespoon fresh or dried juniper berries
2 tablespoons fresh thyme leaves, or 2 teaspoons dried thyme
1 tablespoon minced fresh sage, or 1 teaspoon dried sage
1 tablespoon minced fresh marjoram, or 1 teaspoon dried marjoram
1 bay leaf, crushed
½ teaspoon freshly grated nutmeg
Salt
Freshly ground black pepper
½ cup dry white wine
2 eggs, lightly beaten
12 ounces pork fatback, thinly sliced
Juniper berries for garnish
Bay leaves for garnish
Fresh thyme, sage, and/or marjoram for garnish
Aspic, made with beef or veal stock and Madeira (optional)

Fruit-Stuffed Roast Pork

Here's a particularly tasty version of one of my favorite food combinations—fruit and pork.

Preheat the oven to 375° F.

Put the walnuts in a small heavy ovenproof skillet in the oven, stirring frequently, until lightly toasted, about 10 minutes. Pour onto a plate to cool.

Combine the toasted walnuts, prunes, raisins, apricots, ginger, sage, and thyme in a food processor or blender and coarsely chop. Quickly blend in the mustard and 2 tablespoons of the Cognac.

Butterfly the pork and pound it with a mallet or other flat instrument to a uniform thickness. Season with salt and pepper to taste, then spread the stuffing mixture over the meat. Working from one long side of each tenderloin, roll the meat up jellyroll fashion. Wrap each roll in several thicknesses of cheesecloth and tie at 1-inch intervals with cotton string.

In a dutch oven or ovenproof casserole, combine the stock, the remaining Cognac, and the bay leaf, bring to a boil, and add the pork rolls. Cover and transfer to the oven until a meat thermometer inserted into the thickest part of the meat registers 135° F, about 30 minutes. Remove the meat from the pan and let cool to room temperature. Remove the string and cheesecloth and wrap the rolls tightly in plastic wrap or foil and refrigerate overnight.

Return the pork rolls almost to room temperature before carving into ¼- to ½-inch-thick slices. Garnish each slice with mint.

Serves 8 to 10 as a starter.

½ cup walnut pieces
½ cup pitted prunes
¼ cup golden raisins
¼ cup dried apricots
1 1-inch piece fresh ginger, peeled
   and sliced
2¼ teaspoons chopped fresh sage,
   or ¾ teaspoon dried sage
1½ teaspoons fresh thyme,
   or ½ teaspoon dried thyme
2 tablespoons Dijon-style mustard
½ cup Cognac
2 1½-pound boned pork tenderloins
Salt
Freshly ground black pepper
1 cup homemade beef or veal stock
   (page 92), or canned broth
1 bay leaf, crumbled
Tiny fresh mint leaves or shredded
   large mint leaves for garnish

Pork and Ham Pâté in Pastry
(Pâté de Jambon en Croûte)

FORCEMEAT
1 pound boned pork, coarsely
    chopped
8 ounces pork fatback, coarsely
    chopped
3 garlic cloves, minced or pressed
2 tablespoons fresh thyme, or
    2 teaspoons dried thyme
Salt
Freshly ground white pepper

PASTRY
4 cups unbleached all-purpose flour
1 teaspoon salt
¾ cup (1½ sticks) unsalted butter,
    chilled, cut into small pieces
¼ cup shortening, chilled, cut into
    small pieces
1 egg, chilled
About ½ cup iced water

My California touches of fresh vegetables add more color and flavor to this time-consuming but fun-to-make French original.

I didn't specify an amount for truffles; use as many as your taste and budget dictate.

To make the forcemeat, combine the pork, fat, garlic, thyme, and salt and pepper to taste in a bowl. Cover with plastic wrap and refrigerate overnight.

Working in small batches, place the pork mixture in a food processor and chop until smooth. Using a metal dough scraper or wooden spoon, push the mixture through a wire sieve into a bowl and chill for at least 3 hours.

To make the pastry, combine the flour and salt in a food processor or a bowl. Add the butter and shortening and cut in with the steel blade, a pastry blender, or your fingers until the mixture resembles coarse meal. Combine the egg and iced water and blend into the dough just until the mixture holds together; add a little more water if the mixture is too dry to hold its shape. Gather the dough into a ball, wrap in plastic wrap, and refrigerate for at least 1 hour or preferably overnight.

→

6 ounces flavorful baked ham, diced
¼ cup shelled and halved pistachios
3 medium-sized carrots, cut into
    small dice and partially cooked
Fresh or preserved black truffles,
    chopped
4 ounces tender asparagus, blanched
    briefly, chilled in iced water,
    and drained
1 pound boned pork tenderloin,
    trimmed of all fat
1 egg beaten with 1 tablespoon water
    for glazing the dough
Aspic (page 90), made with Madeira
    or sherry, and veal or chicken
    stock

Remove the chilled forcemeat from the refrigerator and mix in the diced ham, pistachios, diced carrots, and truffles.

Roll out the dough into a rectangle about ⅛-inch thick. Using a 1½-quart pâté mold pan as a pattern, cut pieces of dough to line the bottom, sides, and ends. Reserve the remainder for the top and decorations. Grease the mold with butter and line it with the dough; gently press the dough to seal all seams and create a uniform thickness, pressing upward so some excess dough overhangs the rim. Cut the dough to form about a ½-inch collar around all edges. Combine the trimmings with the reserved dough, wrap, and refrigerate until needed.

Fill the dough with about half of the forcemeat mixture, scattering half of the asparagus lengthwise throughout the mixture as you work. Add the pork loin along the middle, gently pressing it into the pork mixture. Cover with the remaining pork mixture, scattering the remaining asparagus throughout. Fold the edges of the dough in over the pâté.

Preheat the oven to 450° F.

Roll out the reserved pastry and cut a strip to cover any remaining area of the pâté not covered with dough and press the seams to join the edges. Brush the dough with the egg glaze. Cut a piece of dough to fit snugly inside the top of the mold and gently press it down to fit over the top of the dough folds, using a dull knife blade to press any overlapping edges down inside the mold. Use a pastry wheel or the tines of a fork to make a decorative design around all edges of the dough, being careful not to cut through the pastry. Using a sharp knife or small cookie cutter, make 2 holes 1 inch in diameter in the top of the pastry to allow steam to escape during cooking and allow aspic to be added later. Roll several thicknesses of foil into tubes 2 inches long and insert to fit inside the air holes to act as chimneys and to prevent juices from leaking onto the pastry during baking. Cut pieces of the reserved dough to decorate around the holes and add any other decorative designs you wish to the top of the pâté. Brush the dough all over with the egg yolk glaze.

Bake for 15 minutes, then reduce the heat to 350° F and continue baking until a meat thermometer inserted into the center of the pâté (not through one of the air vents) registers 150° to 160° F, about 35 minutes. Cover the top loosely with foil if it begins to get too brown. Remove from the oven and cool to room temperature. Remove the pâté from the mold and place on a long platter or tray.

When the pâté is quite cold, prepare the aspic as directed on page 90. Pour about half of it into a bowl, cover with plastic wrap, and refrigerate until very firm; use to chop and surround pâté when serving. Place the remaining aspic in a bowl of iced water. When it is just beginning to set, position a funnel in the foil chimneys and slowly pour in as much aspic as the pâté will hold. Discard the foil chimneys. Wrap the pâté in plastic wrap and refrigerate until the aspic is set, at least 4 hours or as long as overnight.

To serve, slice into ½-inch-thick pieces.

Serves 12 as a starter.

Ham Mousse

Here's a delicious way to use up leftover ham or slices of flavorful ham from the delicatessen. Serve with crisp thin toast or crackers and a dollop of California-style sweet-and-hot mustard.

Pour the Madeira or port into a small saucepan and cook over high heat until the wine is syrupy and reduced to about 2 tablespoons, about 5 minutes. Remove from the heat and reserve.

Beat the egg whites until stiff but not dry; reserve.

Preheat the oven to 350° F.

Place the ham in a food processor and mince until fine. Add the reduced Madeira or port, cream, mustard, and salt, pepper, and nutmeg to taste. Transfer the mixture to a bowl and fold in the beaten egg whites. Turn into a buttered soufflé dish or ovenproof crock, place the dish in a larger pan, and add enough hot (not boiling) water to come halfway up the sides of the dish. Bake until the top feels set to the fingertip, about 35 minutes. Remove from the oven and cool to room temperature, then cover tightly with plastic wrap and chill for at least 2 hours or as long as overnight.

Serves 8 as a first course, or 4 as a main course.

½ cup Madeira or port
4 egg whites
2 cups chopped baked ham
    (about 1 pound)
½ cup heavy (whipping) cream
2 teaspoons California-style
    sweet-and-hot mustard
Salt
Freshly ground white pepper
Freshly grated nutmeg

Decorated Baked Ham

1 12- to 14-pound boned smoked
  ham labeled "precooked" or
  "fully cooked"
⅓ cup Dijon-style mustard
1 cup packed light brown sugar or
  granulated maple sugar
About 4 cups apple cider
Chaudfroid Sauce (page 91), made
  with veal or vegetable stock,
  or Mayonnaise Coulée (page 92)
Fresh herbs for garnish
Pesticide-free edible flowers such as
  borage, roses, or violas
  for garnish
Aspic for coating (page 90), made
  with fruity white wine
Aspic for chopping (page 90), made
  with fruity white wine (optional)

This presentation certainly adds glamour to the ubiquitous baked ham on the buffet.

Preheat the oven to 350° F.

Remove the skin and trim away most of the fat from the ham. Position the ham in a roasting pan and rub the meat all over with the mustard, then sprinkle with the brown sugar. Pour enough apple cider in the pan to come one-third up the sides of the ham. Bake the ham, basting frequently, for about 2 hours, or 30 minutes per pound. Remove from the oven and cool to room temperature, then wrap the ham tightly in plastic wrap and chill until cold or as long as overnight.

Prepare the Chaudfroid Sauce as directed on page 91, or the Mayonnaise Coulée as directed on page 92.

Place the ham on a wire rack in a shallow pan. When the sauce reaches the point of setting, quickly spoon it completely over the ham, bring careful not to create air bubbles. Turn the ham from side to side to coat all exposed surfaces. Refrigerate, uncovered, until the sauce is firm, about 30 minutes.

Prepare the aspic for coating as directed on page 90.

Gently position the decorations on top of the ham to determine desired pattern, then set the decorations aside. Spoon or brush a thin layer of the thickened aspic over the top and sides of the ham as evenly as possible. When the aspic is slightly tacky, grasp the decorations with tweezers, dip them into the liquid aspic, and place them on the ham in the selected pattern. Refrigerate uncovered until the aspic layer sets up, about 15 minutes.

→

Remove the ham from the refrigerator and cover with a second layer of aspic, coating the decorations as well. It may be necessary to repeat with several layers of aspic, chilling for about 15 minutes between each application, to cover the ham and decorations completely. The ham may be served as soon as the final coat of aspic is set or it may be covered with a foil tent that does not touch the ham or decorations and refrigerated for several hours before serving.

To serve, place the ham on a platter and surround it with chopped aspic or more of the same herbs and flowers used to decorate the top.

Serves 18 to 20 as a main dish.

sweets

Summer Berry and Polenta Pudding

An English tradition made with white bread becomes much more flavorful when crunchy Italian-style pound cake is used instead.

To make the cake, preheat the oven to 325° F.

In the large bowl of an electric mixer, combine the butter, powdered sugar, and vanilla extract and beat until creamy. Beat in the eggs and egg yolks, one at a time, beating well after each addition. Fold in the flour and polenta. Pour into 2 greased and flour-dusted 8½ by 4-inch loaf pans and bake until a wooden skewer tests clean when inserted in the center, about 1 hour and 15 minutes. Cool in the pans for about 5 minutes, then turn out onto a wire rack to cool completely.

To make the filling, place the berries in a bowl, sprinkle with the sugar, cover, and let stand at room temperature for several hours or as long as overnight. Pour the berries and resulting juice into a saucepan and place over low heat, stirring gently, until heated through, about 3 minutes. Add sugar to taste, if desired.

To assemble, cut the cold cakes into thin slices. Cut these into wedges and other shapes necessary to fit a lining around bottom and sides of a deep round 5-cup charlotte mold, leaving no spaces between the slices. Spoon the berries and most of the juice into the center, then cover with a layer of the cake pieces; discard the cake crumbs and save any extra pieces for another purpose. Pour the remaining juice over the top. Cover the pudding with plastic wrap, then with a saucer that fits just inside the mold. Place a 2-pound weight on top (canned food works well) and refrigerate overnight.

About 30 minutes before serving, whip the cream until it just holds its shape, season to taste with sugar and almond extract, cover, and refrigerate.

To unmold, run a dull knife blade between the pudding and the mold, cover with a plate, and invert. Garnish with berries and mint and serve in wedges with the almond cream.

Serves 8.

POLENTA POUND CAKE
1⅓ cups unsalted butter, softened
5⅓ cups sifted powdered sugar
2 teaspoons vanilla extract
4 eggs
2 egg yolks
2 cups unbleached all-purpose flour
1 cup polenta or coarse yellow
   cornmeal

BERRY FILLING
4 cups fresh berries—blackberries,
   boysenberries, currants,
   gooseberries, raspberries, or
   strawberries, or a combination
About ¾ cup granulated sugar

ALMOND CREAM
1 cup heavy (whipping) cream
Granulated sugar
Almond extract

Whole berries for garnish
Mint leaves for garnish

Mocha Torte with Raspberry Sauce

MOCHA TORTE

6 ounces unsweetened chocolate
¾ cup (1½ sticks) unsalted butter
4 eggs
2¾ cups granulated sugar
⅛ teaspoon salt
3 tablespoons instant espresso
    powder, preferably Medaglia
    d'Oro
2 teaspoons vanilla extract
¾ teaspoon almond extract
1¼ cups unbleached all-purpose flour
1 cup ground pecans or walnuts

RASPBERRY SAUCE

2 cups raspberries, fresh or
    thawed frozen
Granulated sugar

Powdered sugar for dusting
Fresh raspberries (optional)
Crème fraîche or unsweetened
    whipped cream

Because several versions of a similar recipe for gooey rich brownies exist, I haven't been able to trace the origins of the baking technique I've adapted for this superrich torte. Whoever discovered the technique of chilling not fully cooked dough to turn it into a dense sensation deserves much praise.

Preheat the oven to 425° F. Generously butter a 9-inch round cake pan with a removable bottom, or line a 9-inch round pan with foil, trim the edges of the foil to leave about an inch overhang around the edges of the pan, and generously butter the foil. Set aside.

To make the torte, combine the chocolate and butter in a small saucepan over low heat and stir continuously just until melted and smooth. Remove from the heat and cool.

In the large bowl of an electric mixer, combine the eggs, sugar, salt, espresso powder, and vanilla and almond extracts. Beat at the highest speed until the mixture is very light and creamy, about 10 minutes. Reduce the speed to low, and blend in the melted chocolate mixture just until mixed. Add the flour and nuts and stir just until mixed. Pour into the prepared pan and bake for 35 minutes; the top should be crusty and the center still runny. Cool to room temperature, then cover tightly and refrigerate overnight.

To make the sauce, purée the raspberries in a food processor or blender and add sugar to taste. Strain through a sieve, if desired. Reserve.

To serve, remove the outside ring and bottom of the pan (or use the edges of the foil to lift the torte from the pan; remove the foil). Place the torte on a serving plate, dust the top with powdered sugar, and garnish with whole raspberries, if desired. Serve thin slices with the reserved raspberry sauce and dollops of crème fraîche or whipped cream.

Serves 12 to 16.

Frozen Avocado Lime Pie

The recipe for this refreshing pie came to my photographer, Patricia Brabant, from the jungles of Mexico.

To make the crust, combine the crushed macaroons and melted butter in a bowl and stir to blend well. Press into a 10-inch pie pan and chill while you prepare the filling.

Beat the egg whites until stiff but not dry; reserve.

Peel and pit the avocados, then purée the flesh in a food processor or blender. Add the lime juice and zest, sugar, condensed milk, and egg yolks and blend until smooth. Transfer to a bowl and fold in the egg whites. Pour into the chilled crust, wrap tightly in plastic wrap or foil, and freeze at least 4 hours or as long as 2 days.

To serve, thaw for about 15 minutes, then garnish with lime slices and strawberries, and slice into wedges.

Serves 8 to 12.

1 13-ounce package coconut macaroons, crushed
½ cup (1 stick) unsalted butter, melted
2 eggs, separated
3 ripe avocados
Juice of 6 limes
1 teaspoon grated lime zest (peel with no bitter white pith)
½ cup granulated sugar
1 cup sweetened condensed milk
Lime slices for garnish
Strawberries for garnish (optional)

Coffee and Vanilla *Gelati* Dome with Bittersweet Chocolate Sauce

PEANUT BUTTER SPREAD
½ cup light corn syrup
⅓ cup crunchy peanut butter,
    at room temperature
1 tablespoon unsalted butter
1 egg, at room temperature, lightly
    beaten
½ teaspoon vanilla extract

1 pint homemade or good-quality
    commercial coffee *gelato*
    or rich ice cream

CRUST
1 cup chocolate wafer crumbs
    (about 24 medium-sized wafers)
¼ cup firmly packed brown sugar
½ teaspoon ground cinnamon
6 tablespoons unsalted butter, melted

2 cups homemade or good-quality
    commercial vanilla *gelato*
    or rich ice cream

**BITTERSWEET CHOCOLATE
SAUCE**
8 ounces bittersweet chocolate,
    chopped
2 tablespoons unsalted butter
1 cup heavy (whipping) cream
1 teaspoon vanilla extract

Chocolate-covered coffee beans for
    garnish (optional)

Either make your own smooth Italian-style ice cream from a favorite recipe or purchase a high-quality ice cream that's rich in butterfat. If you prefer a sweeter sauce, use part or all semisweet chocolate instead.

To make the peanut butter layer, combine the corn syrup and 2 tablespoons water in a saucepan and bring to a boil over medium-high heat. Reduce the heat to medium and cook for 5 minutes. Using a wire whisk, beat in the peanut butter until fairly smooth, then stir in the butter until melted and remove from heat. Slowly stir about 2 tablespoons of the mixture into the beaten egg, then add the egg mixture to the saucepan. Place over low heat and simmer until the egg is cooked, about 2 minutes. Remove from the heat and stir in the vanilla. Cover and refrigerate until spreadable, about 30 minutes.

Soften the coffee *gelato* until it reaches spreadable consistency. Spread in an even layer up to the rim of a 5-cup rounded mold or bowl. Cover tightly with plastic wrap and freeze until the ice cream is firm.

Remove the mold from the freezer and spread the peanut butter mixture evenly over the coffee *gelato* layer. Cover tightly with plastic wrap and freeze until firm.

To make the crust, combine the chocolate wafer crumbs, brown sugar, and cinnamon in a mixing bowl. Add the melted butter and blend well with a fork. Reserve.

Soften the vanilla *gelato* until it reaches spreadable consistency. Remove the mold from the freezer and spread the vanilla *gelato* evenly over the peanut butter layer. Cover with an even layer of the cookie mixture, wrap tightly in foil, and freeze until firm or as long as overnight. Remove from the freezer about 15 minutes before serving.

→

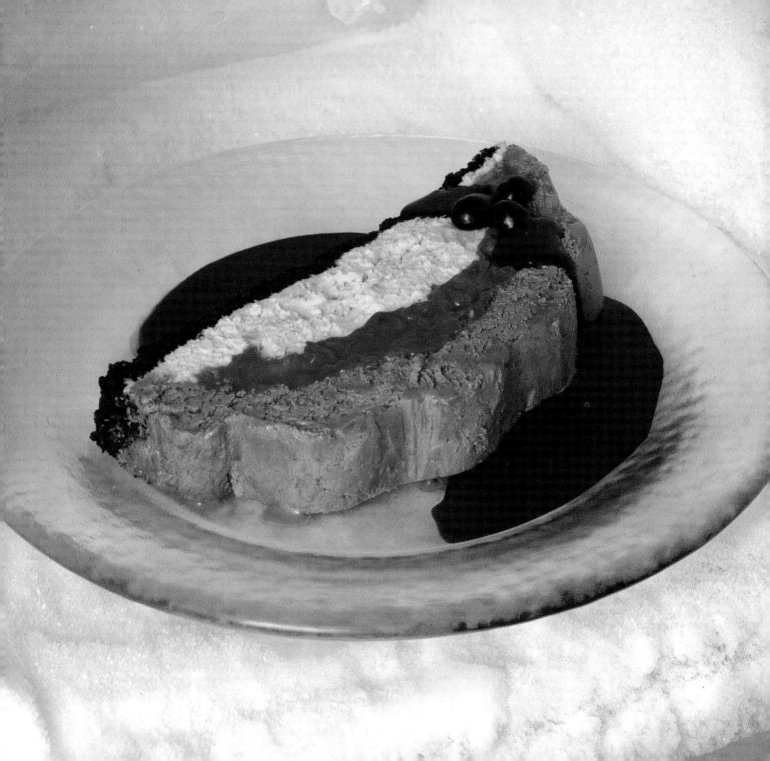

To make the sauce, combine the chocolate, butter, and cream in a saucepan over low heat and cook, stirring frequently, until the chocolate is melted and the mixture is smooth. Stir in the vanilla extract and cool to room temperature, or refrigerate, then reheat just to warm before serving.

To unmold the dome, dip the mold or bowl briefly in a container of hot water, then invert the ice cream onto a plate. Drizzle some of the chocolate syrup over the top and garnish with the coffee beans. To serve, slice in wedges and serve each slice with additional sauce.

Serves 6 to 8.

basics

Aspic

When aspic cools to a honey consistency, it can be used to line molds or add a glistening coat to chilled foods. Or it can be poured into a rectangular pan and chilled until firm, then chopped to surround cold dishes for a shimmering or elegant effect.

Aspic tastes best when homemade stock is used, but when you don't have time to make it, check the freezer shelves of the supermarket for stocks. Canned chicken or beef broth, preferably the low-sodium type, is acceptable, but you'll probably want to dilute it some with water. Dried cubes of beef, chicken, or vegetable stock can be reconstituted with additional water to produce a flavorful aspic stock.

To make an amber-colored, spirited aspic, substitute Cognac or brandy for the wine. To make a clear uncolored aspic, substitute half water and half dry white wine for the stock or broth and add clear spirits, such as vodka or gin, to taste if you wish.

3 tablespoons (3 envelopes) unflavored gelatin
1 quart light homemade chicken, veal, fish, or vegetable stock, clarified (page 93)
½ cup white wine, sherry, Madeira, or port

Combine the gelatin and stock in a small saucepan and let stand until the gelatin is soft, about 5 minutes. Place over medium heat and stir until the gelatin dissolves, about 2 minutes. Remove from heat and stir in the wine.

To use as a coating, pour the aspic into a bowl and place it in a larger bowl of iced water or in the refrigerator. Stir frequently but carefully (to prevent air bubbles from forming) until the aspic cools to the consistency of honey.

Pour or spoon the aspic over the top of a finished and decorated dish. Refrigerate uncovered until the aspic is set, then cover lightly with plastic wrap. Should the aspic become too thick before the coating is finished, melt and rechill it.

To line a mold with aspic, pour the cooled aspic into the mold, being careful to prevent air bubbles from forming. Place the mold in a bowl of iced water that comes almost to the top of the mold and let stand until the aspic begins to set. Pour off the aspic, leaving a fairly thick layer in the pan. If the aspic is too thin, add more liquid aspic and chill again.

To use aspic as a chopped garnish, pour the aspic into a shallow bowl or pan, and refrigerate until firmly set, at least 4 hours or as long as 2 days. Just before serving, cut the aspic into neat cubes or haphazardly chop it.

Makes 1 quart.

Chaudfroid Sauce

This opaque sauce not only keeps the food underneath moist and longer-lasting by protecting it from air, but adds flavor and hides flaws. More, this smooth covering serves as a background for decorations that can turn simple fare into a fanciful presentation.

Classically, chaudfroid begins with a roux-based sauce. Because it can be tricky to get the sauce to set up without being sticky, most *gardemanger* cooks (specialists in decorative cold foods) now bind the sauce with cornstarch and unflavored gelatin.

6 cups lightly flavored chicken, duck, veal, fish, or vegetable stock, all fat removed
2½ cups light cream (half and half)
5 tablespoons cornstarch
1 tablespoon dry white wine or water
2 envelopes (2 tablespoons) unflavored gelatin
Salt
Freshly ground white pepper (optional)

Place the stock in a saucepan over medium heat and cook until reduced to about 2½ cups, about 20 minutes. Remove from heat.

Place the cream in a small saucepan over medium heat and cook, stirring frequently, until reduced to about 1¼ cups, about 15 minutes. Strain through a fine sieve into the stock. Dissolve the cornstarch in the wine and stir in with the cream.

Return the sauce to medium heat and bring to a boil. Remove from heat and stir in the gelatin until dissolved. Strain the sauce into a bowl, using a fine sieve lined with cheesecloth. Season to taste with salt and pepper. Place the bowl in a larger bowl of iced water and stir gently with a wooden spoon (to avoid forming air bubbles) until the sauce begins to thicken. Spoon over the food to be covered. If the sauce gets too thick before using, it can be melted down and chilled again.

Makes about 1 quart.

VARIATION: To make a pale green chaudfroid, rinse, drain, and mince about 1 pound fresh spinach or thaw 1 10-ounce package chopped frozen spinach. Wrap the spinach in cheesecloth and, working over a bowl, squeeze the cheesecloth to collect as much spinach juice as possible. Strain through a fine sieve to remove any bits of spinach. Stir the juice into the sauce when the gelatin is added.

Mayonnaise Coulée

For the same visual effect as more complicated chaudfroid, use this to mask any dish that's compatible with the flavor of mayonnaise.

2 tablespoons (2 envelopes) unflavored gelatin
2 cups Mayonnaise (adjacent recipe), or good-quality commercial mayonnaise

Stir together the gelatin and ½ cup water in a small saucepan and let stand until the gelatin is soft, about 5 minutes. Place over medium-high heat and stir until the gelatin melts, about 2 minutes. Remove from heat and cool to room temperature.

Blend the cooled gelatin well into the mayonnaise. Spoon or pour over the cold food, using several coats if necessary to create a smooth covering.

Makes 2 cups.

Mayonnaise

Homemade mayonnaise may be refrigerated in a covered container for up to 5 days.

1 whole egg, at room temperature
2 egg yolks, at room temperature
1 tablespoon Dijon-style mustard
3 tablespoons freshly squeezed lemon juice or white wine vinegar
2 cups safflower or other vegetable oil, or part olive oil, preferably extra-virgin
Salt

In a food processor fitted with a metal blade or in a blender, combine the egg, egg yolks, mustard, and lemon juice or vinegar. Blend at high speed for about 30 seconds. With the motor running, add the oil in a slow, steady stream. When mayonnaise thickens, turn the motor off. With a rubber or plastic spatula, scrape any oil clinging to the sides of container and mix gently into mayonnaise. Add salt to taste.

Makes about 2 1/2 cups.

Stock

Flavorful stock is the key to good poaching of foods that will be served cold and is essential to aspics and chaudfroid sauce for covering and decorating chilled foods.

For fish stock, use pieces of fresh fish or trimmings and bones.

For chicken stock, use a fat hen, whole fryer, or chicken pieces saved from other cooking, including giblets.

For beef or veal stock, use chunks of fresh meat and/or trimmings and bones.

For vegetable stock, omit the meat and increase the quantity of vegetables, adding other favorite vegetables or their leftover cooking liquids.

Vary the type of herbs to fit the dish you plan to prepare with the stock. For example, tarragon or dill go great with fish.

4 to 5 pounds fish, poultry, or meat, including trimmings and bones
4 carrots, cut into 2-inch pieces
2 celery stalks, cut into 2-inch pieces
2 large onions, each studded with 2 whole cloves
2 leeks, split lengthwise and washed (optional)
4 fresh parsley sprigs
2 or 3 fresh thyme sprigs
2 bay leaves
Salt

Place the fish, poultry, or meat in a heavy stockpot, add enough water to cover by about 2 inches, and bring to a boil over medium heat. Skim off any scum that rises to the surface. Add the carrots, celery, onions, leeks, parsley, thyme, bay leaves, and salt to taste. Return to a boil, reduce the heat, cover, and simmer until meat and vegetables are very tender and the liquid is quite flavorful, about 2 to 3 hours, skimming as necessary. Cool the stock.

Remove any fat on the surface of the cooled stock. Discard the fish, poultry, or meat, or use for another purpose. Discard the vegetables and herbs and strain the stock. Use immediately or store in the refrigerator for up to 4 days.

To freeze stock, first chill overnight, then remove all accumulated fat from the top. Pour into small freezer containers and freeze for up to 6 months.

Makes about 2 quarts.

NOTE: For a more concentrated stock, boil the stock until it is reduced to about one-third of the original volume, cool, and pour into ice trays. Freeze until solid, then transfer the frozen stock cubes to a plastic freezer bag. For use, combine thawed cubes with water to reconstitute stock to desired strength.

Clarified Stock

Removal of all fat particles is necessary for stocks used to make clear aspics.

½ cup egg whites (from 3 or 4 large eggs)
1 quart cold stock

Beat the egg whites and combine with the stock in a saucepan placed over high heat. Bring to a boil, beating continuously with a wire whisk to prevent the egg whites from solidifying. Reduce the heat to low and simmer, beating frequently, until the egg white has absorbed all fat and tiny particles from the stock, about 30 minutes. Strain the clear broth into a bowl through a sieve lined with a paper coffee filter or several layers of cheesecloth.

Makes about 1 quart

Index

ACKNOWLEDGMENTS

To Martha Casselman for her above-duty negotiations as my literary agent.

To the entire staff of Chronicle Books for their continued efforts in printing, distributing, and promoting my work.

To Mary Val McCoy for the careful testing of recipes and great help in the photography studio kitchen.

To Gail High for all her cutting up in the studio kitchen.

To Stephen Suzman for sharing recipes and prolific ideas.

To Scottie McKinney for sharing her secrets of working with aspic and mayonnaise coulée and for decorating the ham on page 77.

To Burt Tessler and James Wentworth of Dishes Delmar, San Francisco, for the loan of 1930s Manhattan glass for photography.

To Patricia Brabant for another stunning collection of photographs. And to her assistants Shari Cohen and Seth Affoumado for all their help in keeping Patricia and me going.

To Cleve Gallat and Peter Linato of CTA Graphics for another fine job of producing the typography and mechanicals.

To my partner Lin Cotton who encouraged me to do this book even though he dislikes most fancy cold food.

And, as always, to my Rockpile Press crew—Addie Prey, Buster Booroo, Joshua J. Chew, Michael T. Wigglebutt, and Dweasel Pickle—for their fine work and great companionship.